IN
STYLE

*Celebrating
Fifty Years
of the
Costume
Institute*

Jean L. Druesedow

DIRECTOR'S NOTE

Judgments of taste tend to be made between two opposing points of view: Apollonian restraint vies with Dionysian exuberance for dominance, and it is the fashion of the day that determines the victor. The degree to which one or the other triumphs in matters of dress, where the urge to change is pronounced, is very much tied to novelty; but fashion is complex, and in its continuing series of maneuvers it rarely reaches either extreme. This contest can be seen in the varying emphasis on form and ornamentation illustrated in the following pages by costumes spanning almost three centuries of fashionable dress. Both this publication and the exhibition it accompanies reveal through some of the most splendid examples in the Museum's collection the taste of the moment of a costume's creation, and thereby the balance struck between the two tendencies at that moment. In each example the finest materials and craftsmanship are present, whether the item is finished simply in lustrous silks of brilliant hue or intricately with dazzling embellishment of woven patterns and applied decoration. Man has a need to ornament, to decorate, and to make his works attractive, and by so doing, he can express the finest aspirations of his time. These works, then, become objects worthy of collection.

Costume clearly demonstrates that functional qualities are no impediment to the creation of art. As with a chair or sconce in the eighteenth-century Wrightsman rooms, or even with a masterful narrative altarpiece serving to describe the Scriptures, form and ornament can be seen to combine very effectively with function to reveal both the art and the artifice of the time: art through its expression of what is considered beautiful; artifice through the calculated effect on the beholder. If such effects were not sought, then why suffer women to be corseted throughout the centuries or why beribbon generals in Louis XIV's France. Costume helps to inform us closely of the ethos of a particular generation, and for the Metropolitan Museum costume completes the study of man and what he makes for his aesthetic subsistence.

The strongest advocate for the full incorporation of costume within The Metropolitan Museum of Art was Polaire Weissman, who directed the growth of the Costume Institute from its founding in 1937, through its merger with the Museum in 1945, to her retirement in 1971. Subsequently, she worked tirelessly in its behalf until her death on November 11, 1986. Her dream of a publication devoted to the costume collection of the Metropolitan has now been realized through the combined efforts of the Costume Institute Staff, and particularly Jean L. Druesedow, Associate Curator-in-Charge, who selected the costumes, supervised their display and photography, and provided the text.

Philippe de Montebello
Director

Reprinted from *The Metropolitan Museum of Art Bulletin* (Fall 1987) © 1987 by The Metropolitan Museum of Art. Designed by Alvin Grossman

Front and back covers: White cotton dresses made for a woman and child about 1818 (p. 28). Detail of an embroidered front section of a man's coat ready to be cut and sewn (p. 22). **Inside covers:** Microphotography of two tulle ball gowns by Christian Dior embroidered with iridescent paillettes and sequins (p. 60)

INTRODUCTION

The costumes in the collection of the Costume Institute were created to be worn by real people in real times and real places. In fact, the word *costume*, which has been used to denote clothing only since the eighteenth century, ultimately derives from the Latin *consuetudo*, meaning "custom" or "usage." In a museum context, costumes are three-dimensional objects that are allied to the other decorative arts but combine both function and beauty. In a collection as rich and diverse as that of the Costume Institute, the social and historical implications of costumes make them important records of their civilizations. Depending upon its cultural context, a costume can reveal the age, sex, and religion and the marital, economic, social, and political status of the wearer, as well as its own geographical origin plus much other data more subjective and psychological in nature. Considered within its aesthetic and cultural context, a garment can give us vivid and intimate glimpses both of the artist who created it and of its wearer.

The formal study of costume began in 1589 or 1590, when Cesare Vecellio (ca. 1530–1600) published in Venice a book illustrated with figures representing peoples of different lands. Travelers' diaries and journals had also recorded examples of dress, some exotic and some simply variations of European clothing. In the eighteenth century the Englishman Joseph Strutt (1749–1802) published several volumes of drawings documenting costumes depicted in works of art, and these volumes became the sources for many nineteenth-century English investigations into the history of dress. The German scholars Karl Köhler (1825–1876) and Max Tilke (1869–1942) published books that advanced the serious study of costume history through evidence found in archaeology, the arts, and extant examples of actual costumes. Such studies continued in the early twentieth century with added emphasis on the sociology of dress. Many museums, including this one, acquired costumes shortly after being founded, but these were primarily collected as textiles or embroideries.

The year 1987 marks the fiftieth anniversary of the founding of the Costume Institute as the Museum of Costume Art, Costume Institute, Inc., by a group of people deeply committed to the concept of costume as art and to the need for a museum in which to study and display it. Its original statement of purpose indicated that this new museum was to include the dress and accessories "of all epochs and all peoples, which may serve industrialists, artists, art historians, craftsmen, and students of all kinds as well as stimulate in the general public an awareness of the importance of dress in the development of the human race and the relation of this field of design to the present and future creative impulses in American life." Among those signing the certificate of incorporation on April 30, 1937, were Irene Lewisohn, who founded and built the Neighborhood Playhouse of the Henry Street Settlement on the Lower East Side of New York, the theater designer Aline Bernstein, who became the first president of the Costume Institute, and Polaire Weissman, who became the executive director. They had all worked closely together at the Neighborhood Playhouse and had acquired an appreciation of the importance of costume in revealing the cultural heritage of the immigrant peoples with whom they worked at the Henry Street Settlement. Irene Lewisohn and her sister Alice Lewisohn Crowley began to collect costumes early in the century, and the idea for a museum of costume was first formalized when the Lewisohns and Aline Bernstein joined a group that organized an exhibition of costume at the Art Center on 57th Street in 1928. The Depression delayed the implementation of the plan for a museum, however, until 1937.

As the reputation of the Costume Institute grew among those using its resources for study, as its collection expanded, and as its exhibitions drew acclaim, the idea was advanced for an association with The Metropolitan Museum of Art. On December 11, 1944, the Museum announced that the Costume Institute would become a branch of the Metropolitan, a move that greatly benefited the field of costume study. A major collection of dress, added to the Metropolitan's own holdings of superb examples, was now to be housed in a context where the art of costume could be studied and exhibited in relation to other arts, and its importance thus could be better understood. The collection brought to the Metropolitan consisted of ten thousand pieces. The first several hundred of these were gifts from Irene Lewisohn, Alice Lewisohn Crowley, and the theater designer Lee Simonson. As early as 1944 Isabel Shults, a devotee of fashion, began a long history of generous donations of costume and endowed acquisition funds for the Costume Institute. Both Lewisohn sisters also provided funds for important acquisitions, many of which are illustrated in this publication. Individual donors of costumes, accessories, library materials, and funds for purchase allow us to continue to expand and improve the scope of our collection, providing ever more opportunities for scholars and the general public to learn from actual examples.

There are three criteria by which a costume is judged before entering the collection. Aesthetic qualities are paramount, and an attempt is made to determine if the costume represents the best use of the elements of costume design by the artist. The placement of the costume in its cultural context helps to determine if it is in the forefront of the design of its time and place. Finally, the condition of the piece indicates whether it can be effectively preserved for future appreciation and understanding. The elements used by an artist who chooses costume as a means of expression—line, color, texture, mass, and movement—can be analyzed for their individual importance in achieving the beauty of the whole. The following questions can be considered: How strong is the line of the silhouette, or the overall shape of the costume? How effective is the use of color, and how does it enhance the quality of the line? Does the texture add to the elements of color and line? Does the mass or volume of each of the preceding contribute to the beauty of the whole? When worn, would the costume be beautiful in motion?

The costumes reproduced on these pages illustrate the broad range of our collection of fashionable Western urban dress. (Another publication would be necessary to encompass the non-Western and regional traditional costumes in the Costume Institute.) No two costumes among the more than forty thousand pieces in the collection are exactly alike, and the sixty-six costumes selected for this publication represent the individuality of their makers and wearers over three centuries. The photographs are arranged in chronological order, beginning with the earliest complete fashionable costume in this hemisphere, an elaborately embroidered dress from about 1695. It is our hope that the costumes shown will illustrate ways in which the history of costume can be studied, the problems of documenting dress, the dangers of the easy assumption that one example represents all possibilities, and the insights into aesthetic and social history that costume can provide. The opportunity to publish this selection is a welcome one, since the fragile nature of costumes prevents any kind of permanent exhibition and mandates that they remain in storage except for special exhibitions of short duration.

As we celebrate the anniversary of the founding of the Costume Institute and look back at the history of the department, we realize how many, many individuals, donors, staff, and volunteers have made possible the achievements of these five decades. Polaire Weissman, who devoted her entire career to the Costume Institute, must be credited with the idea for this publication. It is fitting that we dedicate this volume to her memory and strive to build on her accomplishments in the future.

Jean L. Druesedow
Associate Curator in Charge

NOTES

P. 26, li.10: Betty-Bright P. Low, "Of Muslins and Merveilleuses: Excerpts from the Letters of Josephine du Pont and Margaret Manigault," *Winterthur Portfolio* 9 (1974): p. 29.

P. 33, li. 8: C. Willett Cunnington, *Feminine Attitudes in the Nineteenth Century* (London, 1935), pp. 130–32.

P. 63, li.22: Elizabeth Ann Coleman, *The Genius of Charles James*, exh. cat., Brooklyn Museum (New York, 1982), p. 9.

In a letter dated January 24, 1933, Murray Adams Acton of Acton Surgey Ltd., a London art dealer, informed Joseph Breck, Curator of Decorative Arts and Assistant Director of the Metropolitan Museum, that a dress from the Kimberley Collection in which Breck had expressed interest was available for purchase by the Museum from Acton Surgey. He reminded Breck that the great French costume authority Maurice LeLoir of the Société de l'Histoire du Costume had pronounced it the finest example of its kind extant. Breck acted on the offer, and it was thus that the Museum's earliest complete European costume entered the collection. Made of striped wool embroidered in silver gilt, the dress dates from the very end of the seventeenth century, about 1695, and its only known provenance is Kimberley House, Norfolk, the seat of the Wodehouse family. It is one example from an outstanding group of sixteenth- and seventeenth-century embroideries that were sold from that collection.

The style of the dress, of two pieces, is known as an open robe and petticoat, a fashion followed with minor variations through the end of the eighteenth century. The open robe is drawn away from the front and draped at the back (see p. 7) to reveal the richly decorated petticoat ornamented in an embroidery pattern of French derivation in satin and stem stitches. The thread of silver gilt wound on a yellow silk core is worked perfectly on both sides along the border of the robe and train so that when the skirt is draped the beauty of the embroidery is uninterrupted as it cascades into folds.

Rogers Fund, 1933 (33.54ab)

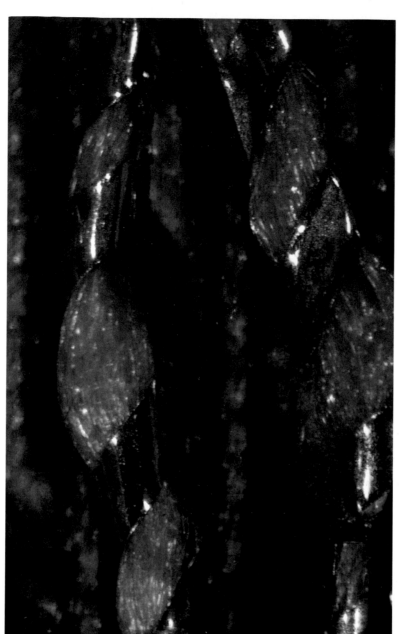

An elliptical hooped under-
skirt known as a pannier
gave this formal gown from the
middle of the eighteenth century
its spectacular width. The
silhouette, which we closely
associate with the century, varied
in width according to fashion
as well as occasion. This costume,
about fifty-five inches wide,
would have been worn at
only the most elaborate social
functions, perhaps at court, or
at a celebration such as a
royal birthday.

Made of silk woven in the
Spitalfields area of London, the
dress is brocaded with three different silver threads. The bottom
detail, taken through a microscope, shows the use of flat silver,
or plate; above is a detail under
even greater magnification that
shows one of the two different
thicknesses of silver wrapped
around a white silk core. The use
of various types of metal thread
gives the sparkling texture to the
brocading.

In this gown the train and skirts
of the open robe have become
so stylized that they form at the
center back only a vestigial hem-
length panel, revealing the entire
expanse of petticoat. The tri-
angular inset at the center front of
the bodice is known as a stomacher. Although this one is made
of matching fabric and ornament,
a stomacher was often prized as a
separate accessory and worn with
a variety of costumes.

Purchase, Irene Lewisohn
Bequest, 1965 (CI 65.13.1abc)

This French dress from the third quarter of the eighteenth century exemplifies the marvelous juxtapositions of patterned textiles and applied decoration so important to the aesthetic of the time. Here a brocaded lace motif winds between floral sprays. The detail of the petticoat shows the wide band of ornament made of ruched ribbons, fly fringe, and rosettes of various shades, all formed into an intricate, richly textured overlay. Fly fringe, used extensively in the eighteenth century, is made of silk threads that have been tied together and clipped so that they form a passementerie of crossed bits of knotted silk branching from a central core. The production of such a dress usually required at least two different craftspeople: the mantua-maker, to sew the dress, and the milliner, to invent and apply the trimmings. Like the two preceding costumes, this is a two-piece dress—a robe and petticoat—but only the front panel of the petticoat remains. Interestingly, a man's waistcoat of the same fabric was acquired at the same time as the dress, and it may have been made from the missing portion of the original petticoat. The erect posture of the eighteenth-century woman, with the shoulders held back, was encouraged by the heavily boned corset, or stays, as well as by the cut of the bodice, the placement of the sleeves, and the tutelage of the dancing master.

Purchase, Irene Lewisohn Bequest, 1959 (CI 59.29.1ab)

Attempting to document costume through the use of paintings is risky since artists' intentions and sitters' wishes often had little to do with the careful rendering of what was actually worn. It is an especially joyful occasion for costume historians when a painting is found that seems to attempt a faithful representation of dress. The above painting by Antoine Raspal depicting what is thought to be his wife's dressmaking shop in Arles around 1760 is of great interest to the Costume Institute because two costumes in the painting are very similar to examples in our collection. The seamstress in the left foreground wears a white petticoat printed in red with a vertical floral motif alternating with solid stripes; this textile bears a striking resemblance to that of the costume pictured on the opposite page, right. The most amazing coincidence, however, is the similarity of the warp-printed silk in our costume (opposite, left) to the petticoat hanging at the left end of the row of dresses in the painting. The colors, the white horizontal stripes, and the spacing and shapes in the patterning are almost identical in the two textiles. The techniques of warp-printing and warp-dyeing, whereby the warp threads are printed or dyed before the cloth is woven, were adapted by the French from the ikat techniques of the Orient and called chiné in Europe after their Eastern origins. Fabric made in this manner is characterized by the softened edges of the design caused by the slippage of the warp threads as they are stretched taut on the loom and during weaving. Both dresses, like the painting, are dated about 1760, and both textiles are also French. Given this correspondence, one wonders how many yards of these textiles were woven for how many dresses, and what the true origins of our costumes might be.

Opposite, left: Purchase, Irene Lewisohn Bequest, 1960 (CI 60.40.2ab). Opposite, right: Rogers Fund, 1937 (37.126.2ab). Above: *Atelier de Couture en Arles*, by Antoine Raspal. Ca. 1760. Collections des Musées d'Arles

The shades of yellow produced in the eighteenth century have a special quality, particularly in heavy saturation. Many different dyestuffs yielded variations of this popular color, and the economics of the textile industry included the export and import of dyes as well as basic fibers, woven cloth, embroidered or painted cloth, and some finished garments. A great number of import-export laws were enacted during the century that protected domestic industry, struck at political adversaries through trade restrictions, and increased revenue through duties. Such laws affected the costumes pictured here. The textile used for the dress on the far left is French and could not legally be imported into England or the American colonies. The English silk of the dress in the center was likewise barred from France but readily exported to the colonies. The dress on this page is made of a hand-painted Chinese export fabric imported to the colonies via England since it was illegal for colonial American merchants to import directly from the source.

Both the textile and the style of the hand-painted dress, said to have belonged to the family of Jonathan Belcher, colonial governor of New Jersey from 1747 to 1757, date from the last third of the century, perhaps the early 1770s, when it became popular to drape the skirt of the open robe into three parts—a style called *à la polonaise*, possibly a reference to the political partitioning of Poland. Various styles have long been named, quite whimsically, after historical times, geographical origins, political events, natural phenomena, and notable or notorious people. The styles of construction of the backs of the dresses pictured were named for their places of origin: the flowing pleats of the dress at the opposite left identified it as a *robe à la française*, while the bodice of the dress on this page has the fullness stitched down in fitted pleats as a *robe à l'anglaise*. Both styles were worn throughout the fashionable world, and both could have their skirts draped *à la polonaise*.

Opposite, left: Purchase, Irene Lewisohn Bequest, 1964 (CI 64.31.1ab). Opposite, right: Purchase, Irene Lewisohn Bequest, 1975 (1975.206.2ab). Left: Gift of Heirs of Emily Kearny Rodgers Cowenhoven, 1970 (1970.87ab)

A source of frustration to scholars is the anonymity surrounding the creation of the majority of historic costumes in existence. In cases where the design and craftsmanship are of superlative quality, the desire to know who made the piece is particularly acute. In 1966 the waistcoat on the opposite page was purchased with Irene Lewisohn Bequest funds from Cora Ginsburg, of Ginsburg and Levy, who had acquired the piece at auction in London. Polaire Weissman, then Executive Director of the Costume Institute, began to research the new acquisition for the Museum's *Annual Report,* and in the 1958 *Bulletin of the Needle and Bobbin Club* she discovered an illustration of a design (right) by Anna Maria Garthwaite for a waistcoat that looked identical. The original design, in the collection of the Victoria and Albert Museum in London, had been acquired by that institution with several volumes of Garthwaite's designs and had been published in articles by Peter Thornton and Natalie Rothstein on the Huguenot silk-weaving industry in London. The marvel of this original design is that it identifies not only the artist, but also the weaver, Peter Lekeux, and gives the date of the sale—October 23, 1747—as well. In addition, the metal threads to be used in the weaving are described: "dark yellow plate," a plain metal strip; "light yellow plain," a metal strip wound around a silk or linen core; and "gray frosted," a textured thread that sparkled. Both Anna Maria Garthwaite (1690–1763) and Peter Lekeux (1716–1768) were important contributors to the English silk industry in the Spitalfields area of London. Garthwaite supplied designs of many sorts. Peter Lekeux rose to the office of Upper Bailiff, the highest in the Worshipful Company of Weavers, the oldest livery company, or craft association, in London. Both the waistcoat and the design were exhibited in 1984 in the *Rococo* exhibition at the Victoria and Albert and published in the accompanying catalogue with entries by Natalie Rothstein.

Opposite: Purchase, Irene Lewisohn Bequest, 1966 (CI 66.14.2). Right: Design for a waistcoat, by Anna Maria Garthwaite. 1747. Victoria and Albert Museum (5985.13)

Mr Lekeux. Octor 23 1747

Dark Yellow plate
Light Yellow plain
Gray Frosted

en's formal suits, like women's dresses, varied in style and ornamentation according to the nature of the occasion. This coat, part of a formal suit, was most certainly worn only at a very special event.

Over time it has suffered types of deterioration often confronted in the conservation of costume. Because costumes are three-dimensional objects, usually made up of a number of different materials, any one component may interact with the others physically, chemically, or both. In this instance the mordant used to dye the black silk from which the velvet was woven embrittled the fibers and caused their disintegration. Likewise, the threads holding the jeweled ornament to the velvet have broken. Careful study under the microscope was necessary to determine the types of stitches and their direction so that the ornament could be restitched and laid properly in place. The detail opposite, photographed through the microscope, shows the complex construction of the glass-and-metal decoration.

Gift of Henry Dazian, 1933 (33.124.2ab)

One of the most popular forms of men's dress in the eighteenth century was the banyan, a robelike informal costume that tended to be more loose and flowing than the other fashionable clothes of the period. The garments were also known as night gowns, dressing gowns, and India gowns—names that reflect both the informality and the Eastern origins of the style. During the first part of the eighteenth century, the banyan seems to have been cut more like a caftan, in a T-shape, without set-in sleeves or other tailored shaping. The second part of the century saw more tailoring applied to the garment. Although considered "undress" as opposed to "formal dress," the banyan was certainly meant to be worn in public as well as in private. Many references in both portraiture and literature attest to its ubiquitous presence.

The center costume on the opposite page, an example of the caftan shape dating from about 1730, was made from an exquisitely patterned compound silk similar to those woven in the 1720s.

Both of the other banyans shown date from approximately fifty years later and are much more tailored in construction, losing some of the comfort associated with the earlier, more commodious style. Artists seem to have favored portraits of men wearing banyans, in part because the garment afforded ample opportunity for drapery painting. In the pair of porcelains above, the artist has used the voluminous banyan to excellent advantage in depicting movement in an amorous encounter. Such works of art aid our understanding of what the banyan might be like in motion.

Above: *Thrown Kiss*. Models by Johann Joachim Kändler. December, 1736. German, Meissen. The Jack and Belle Linsky Collection, 1982 (1982.60.311,312). Opposite, left to right: Catharine Breyer Van Bomel Foundation Fund, 1978 (1978.135.1). Gift of Chester Dale, 1953 (CI 53.74.7ab). Purchase, Irene Lewisohn Bequest, 1956 (CI 56.5.lab)

The fabrication of men's clothing in the eighteenth century involved a number of separately organized crafts: the textile designer, the weaver, the embroiderer, the mercer, and the tailor would all have contributed to the costume illustrated on this page. For an extraordinary suit the customer might specify the colors, applied decoration, and styling at each step of the process. More commonly, workshops would provide a variety of already embroidered fabrics for a customer's consideration. The panel pictured on the opposite page, right, is an example of what such a customer might purchase. This is one of the two front sections of a man's coat embroidered *à la disposition*—that is, in the shape of the finished piece, ready to be cut to fit and sewn. Other pieces for this suit, including collar, cuffs, waistcoat fronts, and breeches kneebands, are also part of the Costume Institute's collection. The small embroidered circles on the upper right of the panel are for covered buttons. Suits *à la disposition* were often made for export. The skill of the embroiderer can be seen in the microscopic details on the opposite page, left. Such magnification shows the luster of the silk threads as well as the minute stitches, especially the French knots, that the professional embroiderers used to create intricate color shadings and patterns.

The formal suit at the left, an example of those made or worn with a contrasting waistcoat, handsomely shows the richness of embroidery added to the luxury of patterned silk velvet. The height of the collar and the narrowness of the sleeves, cuffs, and coat fronts place this suit in the fourth quarter of the century. Suits of this general type were retained for court wear well into the nineteenth century.

Opposite: Purchase, Irene Lewisohn and Alice L. Crowley Bequests, 1982 (1982.290d). Left: Rogers Fund, 1932 (32.35.12abc)

The yellow-and-white striped overdress at the center of this page was part of Irene Lewisohn's initial gift to the new Museum of Costume Art, Costume Institute, Inc., in 1937. Formerly part of a collection belonging to Roy Langford of London, it represents the silhouette of the late eighteenth century and is very like many dresses illustrated by Nicholas Heideloff in the *Gallery of Fashion* (opposite; April 1, 1795). With such publications at the end of the century, fashion journalism began. The white gown on this page, right, is also typical of the time. Known as a round gown because it is one piece and closed in front, as opposed to the open robe and petticoat fashionable previously in the century, it is made of the sheerest cotton called mull, imported from India throughout the eighteenth century and into the nineteenth.

The man's coat, with high collar, wide lapels, and narrow tails, represents the extreme of late eighteenth-century male fashion, when striped silks predominated.

Left to right: Purchase, Irene Lewisohn Bequest, 1968 (CI 68.68.2). Gift of Irene Lewisohn, 1937 (CI 37.46.1). Gift of the Grace Ziebarth Collection, 1976 (1976.142.1). Opposite: The Elisha Whittelsey Collection, The Elisha Whittelsey Fund, 1950 (50.611.1[2])

Fig. 48.   Fig. 49.   Fig. 50.

Published as the Act directs April 1.1795, by N.Heideloff, at the Gallery of Fashion Office, N.º90, Wardour Street.

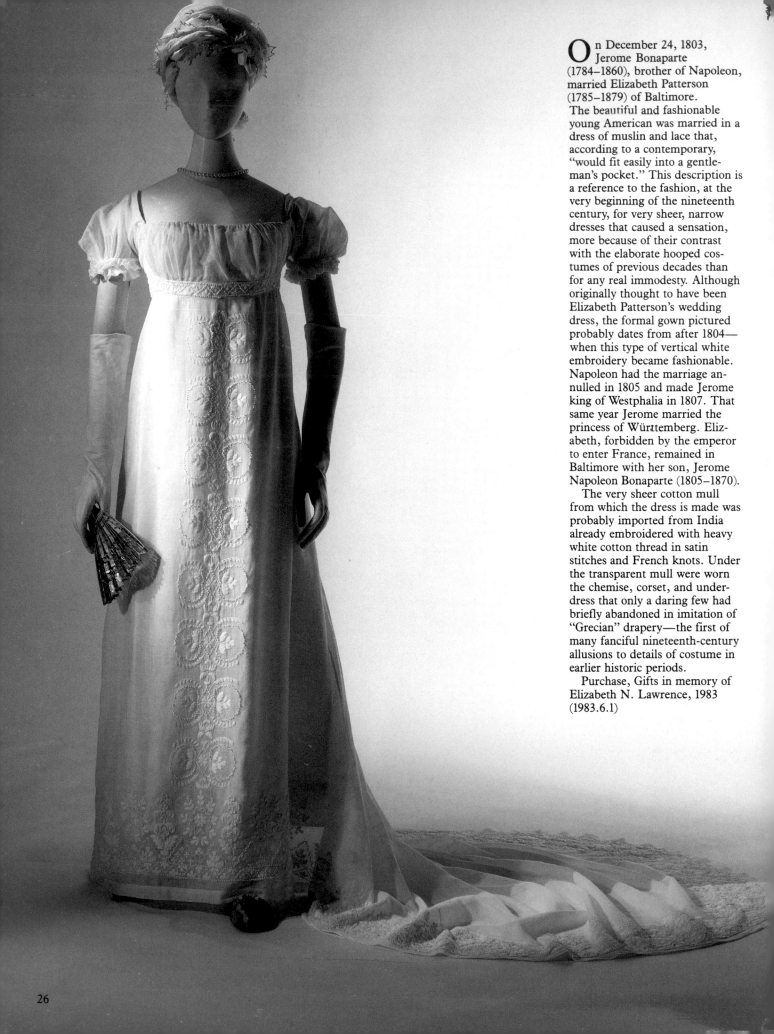

On December 24, 1803,
Jerome Bonaparte
(1784–1860), brother of Napoleon,
married Elizabeth Patterson
(1785–1879) of Baltimore.
The beautiful and fashionable
young American was married in a
dress of muslin and lace that,
according to a contemporary,
"would fit easily into a gentle-
man's pocket." This description is
a reference to the fashion, at the
very beginning of the nineteenth
century, for very sheer, narrow
dresses that caused a sensation,
more because of their contrast
with the elaborate hooped costumes of previous decades than
for any real immodesty. Although
originally thought to have been
Elizabeth Patterson's wedding
dress, the formal gown pictured
probably dates from after 1804—
when this type of vertical white
embroidery became fashionable.
Napoleon had the marriage an-
nulled in 1805 and made Jerome
king of Westphalia in 1807. That
same year Jerome married the
princess of Württemberg. Elizabeth, forbidden by the emperor
to enter France, remained in
Baltimore with her son, Jerome
Napoleon Bonaparte (1805–1870).

The very sheer cotton mull
from which the dress is made was
probably imported from India
already embroidered with heavy
white cotton thread in satin
stitches and French knots. Under
the transparent mull were worn
the chemise, corset, and under-
dress that only a daring few had
briefly abandoned in imitation of
"Grecian" drapery—the first of
many fanciful nineteenth-century
allusions to details of costume in
earlier historic periods.

Purchase, Gifts in memory of
Elizabeth N. Lawrence, 1983
(1983.6.1)

In fashion the Romantic movement took hold just after the beginning of the nineteenth century. By 1810 more applied decoration was to be found at hemlines, and as the first quarter of the century progressed, sleeves began to widen, as seen on this and the opposite page.

The white cotton costumes for the woman and child at the left date from about 1818. The adult's dress is a fine muslin with inset mull puffs, while the child's dress is entirely of mull. A fashion illustration from *La Belle Assemblée*, an English fashion periodical of that date, shows a dress ornamented with similar tiny puffs at hem, cuffs, and neckline and describes it as a "déshabille walking dress."

Left to right: Purchase, Marcia Sand Bequest, in memory of her daughter, Tiger (Joan) Morse, 1981 (1981.13.3). Purchase, Irene Lewisohn Bequest, 1982 (1982.183.1)

Of the dresses pictured on these two pages, the earliest is the yellow silk on this page, left, which was probably made late in the first decade of the 1800s; the woolen shawl, a style popularized by the empress Josephine, is a French version of those from Kashmir. The sleeve of the green and white spencer jacket of the other costume indicates a date from the second decade, as does the decoration at the hem. This dress, made of a fine silk net called maline, was badly disintegrated when acquired by the Costume Institute. During careful restoration over several years, the original ornament was meticulously charted and couched to a new silk maline skirt. The small urn-shaped purse and the turbanlike hats are examples of the combination of stylistic elements found often in costume—in this case, Neoclassicism mixed with developing Romanticism.

Left to right: Rogers Fund, 1937 (37.116a). Purchase, Irene Lewisohn Bequest, 1985 (1985.222.2ab)

The pinnacle of the Romantic movement in dress was reached around 1830. The silhouette had made the transition from the columnar to the X-shape, wide at shoulder and hem and narrow at the natural waistline. Hairstyles were complex combinations of curls, braids, ribbons, and ornaments. The sleeve had grown steadily into the gigot, or "leg of mutton." As the 1830s progressed, the greatest fullness of the sleeve dropped increasingly toward the elbow. These full sleeves were supported by armbands puffed with down.

Children's clothing generally mirrors elements of fashionable adult dress. The little girl and boy on these two pages both wear very full sleeves, and she is dressed in a shorter, simplified version of adult dress. He wears a "skeleton" suit, an enduring type of clothing for little boys worn from the late eighteenth century well into the twentieth. Such suits, of one or two pieces with numerous buttons in necessary places, have enough fullness to allow movement yet maintain a reasonably tidy appearance.

A fashion plate such as the one on this page from *Petit Courrier des Dames* of April, 1832, shows the idealized and fashionable attitude and dress of the time through the posture and expression of the figures. Accessories, fabrics, dressmakers, and the Parisian shops where they could be found are indicated in the text.

Right: Woodman Thompson Collection, Irene Lewisohn Costume Reference Library. Opposite, left to right: Catharine Breyer Van Bomel Foundation Fund, 1980 (1980.409.3). Purchase, Irene Lewisohn Bequest, 1971 (1971.47.lab). Gift of Mrs. James Sullivan, in memory of Mrs. Luman Reed, 1926 (26.250.lab). Gift of M. Winifred and Beatrice F. Hyslop, 1960 (CI 60.11.7)

The delicacy of the printed textiles in the group of costumes from about 1840 on the opposite page is especially evocative of the ideal of femininity at the time, when the romantic exaggeration of the 1830s waned into sentimentality. C. Willett Cunnington describes the fashion as presenting "a demure prettiness, restrained by moral rectitude," with the bonnet "a perfect symbol of meekness and modesty . . . so that a view of the straight and narrow was all that was permitted." Sleeves narrowed, but skirts, supported by multiple underskirts, continued to expand.

By 1850 the bell-shaped hoop appeared, offering relief from the weight of these layers, and by 1856 there were a number of patented "cage" devices, made of flexible hoops of whalebone or metal sewn to cloth tapes and crinoline. The dress on this page was worn over such a cage and was probably intended for afternoon wear.

Opposite, left to right: Funds from various donors, 1978 (1978.88.2). Purchase, Irene Lewisohn Bequest, 1975 (1975.128.9). Purchase, Marcia Sand Bequest, in memory of her daughter, Tiger (Joan) Morse, Leisure Dynamics Foundation Gift, Catharine Breyer Van Bomel Foundation Fund and Mr. and Mrs. Alan Davis Gift, 1982 (1982.56.3). Left: Gift of Mrs. Edwin R. Metcalf, 1969 (CI 69.32.2ab)

A gown for a grand ball is meant to capture all of the magic of the occasion: the fantasy of romance, the essence of fashionable femininity, and the rush of expectation. The gown illustrated here has a youthful delicacy in its design with broad stripes of plain and moiré taffeta brocaded with flowers. Bows of ribbons woven in matching colors decorate the costume, along with multicolored silk fringe typical of the period. The wide skirt would sway gracefully during the dance, although the circumference would necessitate a certain distance between the partners in spite of flexible hoops. On the whole, the dress is very like that worn by Mme Ines Moitessier in the portrait painted by Ingres in 1856 (National Gallery, London). Full evening dress for women in the mid-nineteenth century differed from day wear primarily in the revealing nature of the neckline, which bared fashionably sloping shoulders. The richness of the fabric and the whimsicality of the ornamentation added to the festive appearance.

Gift of Russell Hunter, 1959 (CI 59.35.4ab)

34

Costumes for leisure wear in the nineteenth century differed little in silhouette from those for any other purpose. For example, even though mountain climbing might demand a shorter skirt and sturdy shoes, it was still undertaken with a crinoline. Summer visits to the seaside did require costumes of more practical fabrics that were washable and durable, or at least not easily ruined by sun and salt water. This costume, which was worn by an American, Mrs. Charles Stillman, in the 1860s, is made of white cotton piqué, a fabric with natural body, due to its weave structure, that was very popular for summer dresses. The sewing machine, invented in 1846 and in wide use by the 1860s, made the application of trimmings like the black wool braid, or soutache, on this costume much less time consuming. In Claude Monet's painting *Women in the Garden* (1866, Musée d'Orsay) a woman wears a similar white dress trimmed in black.

Gift of Chauncey Stillman, 1960 (CI 60.6.11ab)

The couple represented here can be imagined walking along the seashore or promenading at a resort like Saratoga Springs in the late 1860s. The man's suit, with all three pieces made of the same wool-and-silk fabric, is of particular interest since its light color and casual styling mark the first significant departure in men's costume from the somber formality established by Beau Brummell at the beginning of the nineteenth century. This kind of informal ensemble, sometimes called a lounge suit, might be worn for leisure activities in the country or while traveling. The woman's costume, of wool gauze, is also casual in styling and typical of seaside or vacation clothing. The loose-fitting jacket and the broad horizontal bands on the lower skirt suggest the jaunty spirit associated with a holiday.

Left: Purchase, Irene Lewisohn Trust Gift, 1986 (1986.114.4abc).
Right: Purchase, Catharine Breyer Van Bomel Foundation Fund and Irene Lewisohn Bequest, 1985 (1985.20.1a–d)

A preference for the plain but luxurious silk taffetas found in so many costumes from the middle of the nineteenth century is associated with the empress Eugénie, who set fashion throughout the reign of Napoleon III. All four of the dresses pictured here reflect the taste for relatively unornamented day wear appropriate for afternoon visits. The dresses also show the greatest circumference the skirt achieved during the nineteenth century, reached between 1865 and 1867. The gray dress is an example of a practical development whereby a costume had two bodices and two belts, one each for day and for evening, both to be worn with the same skirt. The ball bodice, of course, would have a low neckline, short, tight sleeves, and more fanciful decoration. The blue and rust dresses were both purchased in Paris as part of the trousseau of Grace Russell Hooker in 1867. The rust dress was subsequently altered to update it to the bustle style of the early 1870s.

Left to right: Gift of Althea Adams May, 1977 (1977.204.2ab). Gift of Miss Elizabeth R. Hooker, 1962 (CI 62.35.1abc). Gift of Mr. and Mrs. Alfred Easton Poor, 1958 (CI 58.4.4acd). Gift of Miss Elizabeth R. Hooker, 1962 (CI 62.35.2ab)

Worn by Clara Popham Redner upon her marriage to C. Fred Richards in Philadelphia on December 1, 1880, this lovely dress epitomizes the fashionable silhouette of the time as well as the type of wedding dress we now think of as traditional. Bridal dresses were not always white in past centuries (in fact, white might well have been the exception rather than the rule), nor were they worn only once, since many women used the wedding dress as their best dress for as long as possible. Wedding dresses often prove of special interest to costume historians since the wearer and the date are usually known; these two critical items of documentation are lacking for the vast majority of extant costumes. However, because of the special nature of the occasion, a dress made only for a wedding often may have more fanciful or exaggerated details of styling than ordinary day or formal wear. The elaborate pearl ornament of this dress is an example.

Gift of Mrs. H. Lyman Hooker, 1936 (36.117a)

Mr. and Mrs. Andrew Carnegie were among the passengers on the steamship *Fulda* on the night of April 22, 1887, as they departed for their honeymoon in England and Scotland. For her quiet wedding at 8 o'clock that same evening, Louise Whitfield had chosen to wear the gray wool traveling suit pictured on this page. The steamer left only a little more than an hour after the service that had culminated the couple's seven-year courtship. A practical traveling ensemble, this suit consists of a skirt and two bodices for day wear, as well as an extra set of cuffs, collar, and front insert, or plastron, of gold embroidery on a red ground to transform one bodice for a more formal occasion. The dress at the left on the opposite page was worn by Mrs. Carnegie at her reception in New York upon the couple's return in the fall of 1887, and was part of her trousseau. The Scottish costume in the Carnegie tartan was made for her in 1888 for her first summer at Cluny. The very fashionable bustle silhouette of the late 1880s is found in each of these dresses.

Opposite and this page, left to right: Gift of Margaret M. Flockhart, 1968 (CI 68.53.6ab, 7ab, 5abd)

The bustle, having reached its most exaggerated shape in the late 1880s, suddenly deflated at the end of the decade to become little more than a small pad at the center back of the waist. Abruptly the silhouette changed into the "hourglass figure" that we associate with the turn of the century or the Gay Nineties. The sleeve took only slightly longer to grow once again into a full-blown gigot. By 1895 wide shoulders, narrow waists, and wide hemlines were once again in vogue. The aesthetic of both the textile design and dress silhouette of the period is to some extent an exaggeration of earlier ideas. For example, the large scale of the floral pattern in the dress pictured is characteristic of many silk designs of the era, but both the chiné, or warp print, and the floral motif recall eighteenth-century ideas, which have been reinterpreted here to the taste and technology of the late nineteenth century.

Purchase, Irene Lewisohn Bequest, 1981 (1981.21.2ab)

In 1976 Eva Drexel Dahlgren contacted the Costume Institute to inquire about any interest the Museum might have in a gift of dresses that had belonged to her aunt, Elizabeth Drexel, Lady Decies. What treasures were in store as the trunks, only recently brought to New York from Lady Decies's home in Paris, were opened to reveal a collection of evening gowns from Worth, in pristine condition, dating from about 1898.

Charles Frederick Worth (1826–1895), an Englishman, had established the first couture house in Paris in 1858 with his partner M. Bobergh. Each season, models were created in advance to show clients, revolutionizing the business of fashion. Worth gained immediate popularity when he provided dresses for the empress Eugénie, and his house continued to be a favorite of fashionable Americans into the twentieth century.

A superb example in every way, the dress pictured here reflects the aesthetic of the very end of the century, not only in the Art Nouveau pattern of the textile, but in the reverse S-curve of the silhouette. The textile was woven with velvet scrolls on a satin ground, with each section of the skirt patterned to its shape, *à la disposition*, so that the design of the fabric is intrinsic to the dress.

Gift of Miss Eva Drexel Dahlgren, 1976 (1976.258.1ab)

This white lace afternoon dress from 1901 evokes a way of life dramatically different from ours today, although it represents both the mechanization of the modern age and the handwork of previous eras. A narrow machine-made tape, woven loosely, was arranged in various floral and medallion shapes that were then held in place by handworked lace stitches, creating a shaped fabric from which the dress was made. Even rarer than knowing for whom a costume was made is the existence of a photograph of the costume worn by its original owner. We are most fortunate that Winifred Walker Lovejoy presented the Costume Institute with such a photograph of her mother, Winifred Sprague Walker Prosser, at the time that she donated the dress in 1980. Not only does the photograph (opposite) show the lace in excellent detail, but it also reveals the gracious elegance of the period.

Left: Gift of Winifred Walker Lovejoy, in memory of Winifred Sprague Walker Prosser, 1980 (1980.590.1)

48

The four costumes on these two pages represent the transition to one of the most profound changes in the history of women's fashion. As the twentieth century dawned, women, still tightly corseted and encumbered with long skirts, found themselves taking increasingly active roles outside the home. Dress reform and the women's suffrage movement, begun in the second half of the nineteenth century, had made uneven progress as social consciousness rose haltingly. Many women, uncomfortable with change, held on to traditional roles, while others became increasingly active supporters of reforms. During the first decade of the century, skirts were gradually shortened and the more mantailored walking suit continued to develop from its origins in riding apparel. The three suits on the opposite page date, left to right, from 1903, 1909, and 1914, and illustrate the changes in length and silhouette that allowed considerably more comfort and convenience for active women. The advent of the First World War made such convenience a necessity as women, wearing uniforms such as the one on this page, found themselves supporting the war effort in ways not previously imagined.

The impact of World War I on the status and self-image of women in the twentieth century was incalculable. The uniform here of jacket, skirt, and knickers, which the Costume Institute staff initially supposed was for a nurse, serves as an example of the change from which there could be no return, as is underscored by this excerpt from a letter written by the donor, Jane Darlington Irwin, in 1981: "I would like to correct the description of . . . [the] *Motor Corps* uniform of Elizabeth Remsen Thompson. Mother never was a nurse, but knew all about automobile engines—the knickers were for clambering around truck engines—she was born in 1894 and was known as Lightning Liz."

Opposite, left to right: Gift of Irene Lewisohn, 1937 (CI 37.46.8ab). Gift of Irene Lewisohn, 1937 (CI 37.46.69ab). Isabel Shults Fund, 1985 (1985.140.8ab). Left: Gift of Jane Darlington Irwin, 1981 (1981.523.4ab)

SERAIS-JE EN AVANCE ?

Manteau de théâtre de Paul Poiret

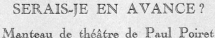

The arrival in Paris during 1909 of Diaghilev's Ballets Russes shook the foundations of established aesthetic sensibilities with the sensuality of the orientalist themes and choreography and the vivid colors of the sets and costumes. No one in the fashion world was affected more than Paul Poiret (1879–1944), whose imaginative use of this inspiration created some of the most outstanding works of twentieth-century fashion design.

By 1910 the silhouette, which had been growing straighter since the beginning of the century, reflected both the new orientalism

and a revised interpretation of early nineteenth-century "classicism." The eclecticism so typical of fashion bloomed as the neckline lowered, the kimono sleeve gained popularity, and the skirt lost its fullness. For Poiret, intensity of color and the unstructured drapery of the kimono and caftan were major design elements, both seen in the coat illustrated here. Among other couturiers, he had experimented with uncorseted shapes, and he credited himself with having done away with the corset—while at the same time binding women at the ankles with the hobble skirt.

This theater coat from 1912 (above right) was among many Poiret designs illustrated by Georges Lepape for the *Gazette du Bon Ton*, an important fashion periodical published between 1912 and 1925. The illustration at the upper left captures the sensuality and luxury of the designer's intention and the social milieu, while the photographs of the actual coat demonstrate the rich colors and textures of the fabrication.

Opposite and above right: Purchase, Irene Lewisohn Trust Gift, 1982 (1982.350.2). Above left: Illustration by Georges Lepape from *Gazette du Bon Ton* (November, 1912)

The spirit and style of Coco Chanel (1883–1971) immeasurably influenced the development of women's fashion in this century. It was Chanel who ultimately understood what the century's far-reaching changes in life style would mean for women and how clothing could accommodate them. Long envious of the practicality, ease, and good design of tailored men's apparel and also realizing the need for even greater freedom of movement in women's clothes, Chanel often used knitted fabrics as well as less-structured tailoring in her innovative early designs. At the same time she was able to enhance elegance and femininity. The costumes pictured below—dating from, left to right, the 1920s, 1930s, and 1950s—represent three decades of her work, yet any of the three could be worn as easily in the 1980s.

An example of Chanel's uncomplicated structure is illustrated in the detail on the opposite page. The coat fronts, collars, and cuffs have no facings. Raw edges were simply turned over once and stitched with several rows of machine stitching, a detail repeated on the body of the coat simply for decoration, or else the selvage edge alone was used, as on the coat center fronts. The lining, which matches the dress, was very carefully and delicately stitched by hand to the coat so that the stitches are not visible on the exterior. Fashions from Chanel combined such remarkably skilled craftsmanship with a simplicity of line to give the twentieth-century walking suit its most enduring and modern form.

Left to right: Isabel Shults Fund, 1984 (1984.31abc). Gift of Diana Vreeland, 1954 (CI 54.16.2ab). Gift of Mrs. Stephane Groueff, 1976 (1976.370.2abc)

For many women, presentation at the Court of Saint James's constituted a momentous social accomplishment. The requisite ceremonial dress for such an occasion had to meet certain specifications, many reminiscent of earlier centuries. This costume, for example, which was worn by Mrs. George Henry O'Neil, the former Bertha Fadelhan Drake of Harrisburg, for presentation before George V in June, 1928, has a train, headdress, and fan, all made to conform to rules governing the occasion at that particular time. Purchased in Paris from Boué Soeurs, the dress and train are decorated with ribbon flowers (a signature of that design house), reminiscent of the ribbon ornaments of the eighteenth century. Even more direct reflections of that distant century are the side hoops, very like low panniers, that were associated with a fashion created by Jeanne Lanvin called the *robe de style*. The train is detachable so that the dress could quite easily be worn for dancing after the court ceremonies had concluded. Such presentations were discontinued in 1958.

Gift of Mrs. George Henry O'Neil, 1968 (CI 68.48a–e)

If there is one style associated with the 1930s, it is the bias-cut dress perfected by Madeleine Vionnet (1876–1975). By manipulating the degree to which the bias (or diagonal of the fabric) draped vertically on the body, Vionnet created dresses where the inherent structure of the textile gave shape to the dress. The crepe-back satin of the gold dress at the near right is typical of the fabrics Vionnet chose for her designs.

The dress at the far right, from a 1938 collection of floating tulle-and-appliqué skirts over narrow bias-cut underdresses, was originally owned by the Duchess of Windsor. It was one of many dresses solicited in 1940 for a charity fashion show for the French relief effort organized by Mrs. Harrison Williams, Lady Mendl, and Mrs. Ector Munn. Some of these dresses, made by important couturiers for notable women, were exhibited in 1940/41 at the Museum of Costume Art, Costume Institute, Inc., at 630 Fifth Avenue in the *Retrospective Exhibition of the Paris Openings: 1932–1940*. They were given to the collection in 1946.

Left to right: Gift of Mr. and Mrs. Charles Abrams, 1978 (1978.29.2ab). Gift of Mrs. Harrison Williams, Lady Mendl, and Mrs. Ector Munn, 1946 (CI 46.4.24ab)

F ew twentieth-century costumes, when viewed as three-dimensional works of art, have the strength of line or the sculptural qualities of those designed by Cristóbal Balenciaga (1895–1972). Although he opened his house in Paris in 1937 and worked in France, there is much in his early work, especially, that shows his Spanish heritage. This costume, called the Infanta dress because of its elliptical hooped skirt—an alleged reference to the Velázquez portrait *The Infanta Margarita* (ca. 1660, Prado)—was part of Balenciaga's 1939 collection. The design's dramatic effect comes from the strong, scrolling pattern of black velvet appliquéd on white satin.

Inset: Photograph by Hoyningen-Huene from *Harper's Bazaar* (September 15, 1939). Dress: Gift of Mrs. John Chambers Hughes, 1958 (CI 58.34.21ab)

During the Second World War, most of the couture houses in Paris either were closed or operated at a minimal level. War shortages affected every aspect of life, particularly the luxury industries. Styles continued to change, however, in spite of the war and sometimes in defiance of it. In the spring of 1947, when Christian Dior (1905–1957) showed his first collection with tight waists and long, full skirts, Carmel Snow, the editor of *Harper's Bazaar*, commented "What a new look!" and gave the style its name. These gowns from the 1949 collection, named Venus (left) and Junon (right) by Dior, shimmer with the resurgent luxury of sequined tulle. Such strapless gowns gained wide popularity in the 1950s.

Left to right: Gift of Mrs. Byron C. Foy, 1953 (CI 53.40.7a–e, 5a–e)

"Shocking pink," the color most closely identified with Elsa Schiaparelli (1890–1973), implies the combination of humor, outrageousness, style, and elegance found in this designer's imaginative work. Surprise is almost always present in her designs—for example, the yellow satin gloves made for the dress at the left, a gift of the designer from her personal wardrobe to the Costume Institute. Well-known artists, including Salvador Dali, sometimes collaborated with Schiaparelli to create costumes and accessories of great vitality and originality. Just as the firm of Rébé did the beading for the Dior dresses on the opposite page, the firm of LeSage did the beading for Schiaparelli, continuing the tradition of applied decoration by specialists such as Rose Bertin, the milliner who decorated Marie Antoinette's dresses.

Left to right: Gift of Schiaparelli, 1951 (CI 51.110.1,2ab). Gift of Alma De Luce, 1975 (1975.139.1ab)

T hree of the most important
designers to emerge in the
American fashion industry were
Norman Norell (1900–1972),
Gilbert Adrian (1903–1959), and
Claire McCardell (1906–1958).
Their designs combined a sense of
comfort, casualness, and ease with
dramatic colors and interesting
textures to create a very sophisti-
cated look. In clothing like the
dress at the above left, Norell gave
to American fashion the quality
craftsmanship of European couture. The same great imaginative
flair that characterized Gilbert
Adrian's Hollywood costumes also
set street fashion and made his
couture creations dramatic. The
dress in the center, called the
Roan Stallion, won him an
American Fashion Critics Award
in 1945. Claire McCardell, who
created the dress on the right,
brought innovative cut and use
of fabrics to mass-produced
clothing. It is to her work that
many of today's designers turn,
looking for inspiration and solu-
tions to the problem of achieving
creative designs within the strict-
ures of mass production.

Left to right: Gift of Mr. and
Mrs. Richard V. Hare, 1976
(1976.372.3ab). Gift of Gilbert
Adrian, 1945 (CI 45.94). Gift
of Claire McCardell, 1949
(CI 49.37.5abc)

Alone among American designers, Charles James (1906–1978) represents the obsession of an artist confronting his materials to seek a singular vision and create shapes independent of fashion. For well over three decades he worked and reworked his concepts to perfect minute details, straining his ideas, his materials, and his clients to their limits. He built his clothes like architecture, draping the outer fabrics over a complex understructure. Of the two evening dresses pictured here, the Four-Leaf Clover, or Abstract, ball gown in the foreground best reflects the sculptural engineering of his work. Versions of the dress in the background were ordered by clients from 1949 to 1972. Balenciaga said that James had raised dressmaking from "an applied art form to a pure art form."

Left to right: Gift of Elizabeth Fairall, 1953 (CI 53.73). Gift of E. J. Taylor, 1975 (1975.185)

CREDITS

Pp. 5–7: Formal dress of gray-brown wool embroidered in silver gilt. English, ca. 1695. Rogers Fund, 1933 (33.54ab)

Pp. 8–9: Formal dress of blue silk brocaded in silver. English, mid-18th century. Purchase, Irene Lewisohn Bequest, 1965 (CI 65.13.1abc)

Pp. 10–11: Dress of lavender-pink silk brocaded in polychrome motifs. French, ca. 1760. Purchase, Irene Lewisohn Bequest, 1959 (CI 59.29.1ab)

P. 12: Dress of mauve shot silk taffeta with chiné polychrome floral pattern. French, 1760. Purchase, Irene Lewisohn Bequest, 1960 (CI 60.40.2ab). Dress of white cotton printed in red. French, ca. 1760. Rogers Fund, 1937 (37.126.2ab)

P. 13: *Atelier de Couture en Arles*, by Antoine Raspal (1738–1811). Ca. 1760. Collections des musées d'Arles.

P. 14, left to right: Dress of yellow silk. French, ca. 1775. Purchase, Irene Lewisohn Bequest, 1964 (CI 64.31.1ab). Dress of pale yellow silk brocaded in polychrome motifs. English, ca. 1765. Purchase, Irene Lewisohn Bequest, 1975 (1975.206.2ab)

P. 15: Dress of yellow Chinese export silk with hand-painted motifs. American, after 1770. Gift of Heirs of Emily Kearny Rodgers Cowenhoven, 1970 (1970.87ab)

P. 16: Design for a waistcoat, by Anna Maria Garthwaite. English, 1747. Pencil, ink, and watercolor. Victoria and Albert Museum (5985.13)

P. 17: Man's waistcoat of blue silk with silver and polychrome silk motifs. English, 1747. Purchase, Irene Lewisohn Bequest, 1966 (CI 66.14.2)

Pp. 18–19: Man's formal suit of black silk velvet embroidered with blue glass and metal. French, 3rd quarter of 18th century. Gift of Henry Dazian, 1933 (33.124.2ab)

P. 20: *Thrown Kiss*. Hard-paste porcelain. Models by Johann Joachim Kändler (1706–1775). December 1736. German, Meissen. The Jack and Belle Linsky Collection, 1982 (1982.60.311,312)

P. 21, left to right: Man's banyan of yellow damask. English, ca. 1780. Catharine Breyer Van Bomel Foundation Fund, 1978 (1978.135.1). Man's banyan and matching waistcoat of predominantly blue and ivory silk. French, ca. 1730. Gift of Chester Dale, 1953 (CI 53.74.7ab). Man's banyan and matching waistcoat of striped silk in blue, ivory, rust, and yellow. European, ca. 1780. Purchase, Irene Lewisohn Bequest, 1956 (CI 56.5.1ab)

P. 22: Man's unconstructed formal suit (*habit à la disposition*) of purple silk with polychrome embroidery. French, ca. 1780. Purchase, Irene Lewisohn and Alice L. Crowley Bequests, 1982 (1982.290d)

P. 23: Man's formal suit of dark brown silk velvet with polychrome embroidery. French, 4th quarter of 18th century. Rogers Fund, 1932 (32.35.12abc)

P. 24, left to right: Man's coat of striped silk in yellow, rust, and blue on olive ground. French (?), ca. 1795. Purchase, Irene Lewisohn Bequest, 1968 (CI 68.68.2). Overdress of striped satin in yellow and white. English, ca. 1795. Gift of Irene Lewisohn, 1937 (CI 37.46.1). Dress of white cotton mull. American, 1797. Gift of the Grace Ziebarth Collection, 1976 (1976.142.1)

P. 25: Engraving by Nicholas Heideloff from *Gallery of Fashion* (April 1, 1795), figs. 48–50. The Elisha Whittelsey Collection, The Elisha Whittelsey Fund, 1950 (50.611.1[2])

Pp. 26–27: Formal dress of white cotton mull embroidered in white cotton. American, ca. 1805. Purchase, Gifts in memory of Elizabeth N. Lawrence, 1983 (1983.6.1)

P. 28, left to right: Dress of white cotton muslin, mull, and lace. European, ca. 1818. Purchase, Marcia Sand Bequest, in memory of her daughter, Tiger (Joan) Morse, 1981 (1981.13.3). Child's dress of white cotton mull. English, ca. 1818. Purchase, Irene Lewisohn Bequest, 1982 (1982.183.1)

P. 29, left to right: Dress of yellow silk. French, ca. 1810. Rogers Fund, 1937 (37.116a). Dress of striped green and white silk and embroidered maline. English, ca. 1820. Purchase, Irene Lewisohn Bequest, 1985 (1985.222.2ab)

P. 30: Plate from *Petit Courrier des Dames* (April

1832). Woodman Thompson Collection, Irene Lewisohn Costume Reference Library

P. 31, left to right: Dress of cream silk printed in green, purple, red, and gold. English, ca. 1837. Catharine Breyer Van Bomel Foundation Fund, 1980 (1980.409.3). Dress of red, blue, and yellow plaid silk. English, ca. 1830. Purchase, Irene Lewisohn Bequest, 1971 (1971.47.1ab). Dress and pelerine of plum-colored silk. American, ca. 1835. Gift of Mrs. James Sullivan, in memory of Mrs. Luman Reed, 1926 (26.250.1ab). Little boy's suit of dark green wool. American, ca. 1833. Gift of M. Winifred and Beatrice F. Hyslop, 1960 (CI 60.11.7)

P. 32, left to right: Dress of white cotton printed in red and pink. American, ca. 1838–40. Funds from various donors, 1978 (1978.88.2). Dress of white cotton printed in lavender and black. English, ca. 1837–40. Purchase, Irene Lewisohn Bequest, 1975 (1975.128.9). Dress of white cotton printed in orange. American, ca. 1844. Purchase, Marcia Sand Bequest, in memory of her daughter, Tiger (Joan) Morse, Leisure Dynamics Foundation Gift, Catharine Breyer Van Bomel Foundation Fund and Mr. and Mrs. Alan Davis Gift, 1982 (1982.56.3)

P. 33: Dress of polychrome ribbon-plaid silk on black ground. American or European, 1850s. Gift of Mrs. Edwin R. Metcalf, 1969 (CI 69.32.2ab)

Pp. 34–35: Ball gown of ivory silk taffeta striped in blue and brocaded in polychrome silks. American, ca. 1860. Gift of Russell Hunter, 1959 (CI 59.35.4ab)

P. 36: Dress of white cotton piqué trimmed with black soutache. American, ca. 1862. Gift of Chauncey Stillman, 1960 (CI 60.6.11ab)

P. 37: Man's suit of beige wool and silk. English, ca. 1865–70. Purchase, Irene Lewisohn Trust Gift, 1986 (1986.114.4abc). Dress of brown and white wool gauze banded in blue, brown, and ecru. English, ca. 1867. Purchase, Catharine Breyer Van Bomel Foundation Fund and Irene Lewisohn Bequest, 1985 (1985.20.1a–d)

Pp. 38–39, left to right: Dress of violet silk faille trimmed with black soutache. American, 1863–65. Gift of Althea Adams May, 1977 (1977.204.2ab). Dress of bright blue silk faille trimmed with matching satin and fringe. French, ca. 1867. Gift of Miss Elizabeth R. Hooker, 1962 (CI 62.35.1abc). Dress of gray silk faille trimmed with gray braid. French, ca. 1865–67. Gift of Mr. and Mrs. Alfred Easton Poor, 1958 (CI 58.4.4acd). Dress of rust silk faille trimmed with brown satin and fringe. French, 1867–71. Gift of Miss Elizabeth R. Hooker, 1962 (CI 62.35.2ab)

Pp. 40–41: Wedding dress of white silk trimmed with pearls. American, 1880. Gift of Mrs. H. Lyman Hooker, 1936 (36.117a)

P. 42, left to right: Dress of coral silk trimmed with brown velvet, gold passementerie. American, 1887. Gift of Margaret M. Flockhart, 1968 (CI 68.53.6ab). Scottish costume of navy blue wool and Carnegie plaid tartan. Scottish, 1888. Gift of Margaret M. Flockhart, 1968 (CI 68.53.7ab)

P. 43: Wedding ensemble of gray wool and beige passementerie. American, 1887. Gift of Margaret M. Flockhart, 1968 (CI 68.53.5abd)

Pp. 44–45: Dress of silk striped in beige and ivory with chiné roses. American, ca. 1895. Purchase, Irene Lewisohn Bequest, 1981 (1981.21.2ab)

Pp. 46–47: Evening dress of black silk velvet voided to white satin ground. French, 1898. Label: Worth, Paris. Gift of Miss Eva Drexel Dahlgren, 1976 (1976.258.1ab)

Pp. 48–49: Dress of white cotton tape-lace medallions connected with needle lace. American, 1901. Gift of Winifred Walker Lovejoy, in memory of Winifred Sprague Walker Prosser, 1980 (1980.590.1)

P. 50, left to right: Dress of red wool with vestee and undersleeves of white silk chiffon and lace. English, ca. 1903. Gift of Irene Lewisohn, 1937 (CI 37.46.8ab). Suit of brown silk trimmed with brown braid. English, ca. 1909. Label: Phillips and Sons, London. Gift of Irene Lewisohn, 1937 (CI 37.46.69ab). Suit of blue silk taffeta. European, ca. 1914. Isabel Shults Fund, 1985 (1985.140.8ab)

P. 51: Motor corps uniform of olive-drab wool. American, 1917. Label: Abercrombie and Fitch, Co., New York. Gift of Jane Darlington Irwin, 1981 (1981.523.4ab)

Pp. 52–53: Theater coat of yellow and pale blue silk charmeuse trimmed with black velvet and silver lace. French, 1912. Designed by Paul Poiret. Purchase, Irene Lewisohn Trust Gift, 1982 (1982.350.2)

P. 53, left: Illustration by Georges Lepape from *Gazette du Bon Ton* (November, 1912), plate VI. Watson Library 233.4 G25

Pp. 54–55, left to right: Ensemble: dress of silk chiffon printed in cerise, orange, and black; coat of yellow-and-gray wool tweed lined in dress fabric. French, ca. 1927. Label: Chanel. Isabel Shults Fund, 1984 (1984.31abc). Suit of blue linen. French, 1937. Label: Chanel. Gift of Diana Vreeland, 1954 (CI 54.16.2ab). Suit of black, blue, and azure tweed. French, ca. 1955. Label: Chanel. Gift of Mrs. Stephane Groueff, 1976 (1976.370.2abc)

Pp. 56–57: Court presentation dress of white net embroidered in silver cord over pink chiffon trimmed with silk ribbon flowers. French, 1928. Label: Boué Soeurs. Gift of Mrs. George Henry O'Neil, 1968 (CI 68.48a–e)

P. 58, left to right: Evening dress of gold silk satin reversing to green crepe. French, ca. 1933. Designed by Vionnet. Gift of Mr. and Mrs. Charles Abrams, 1978 (1978.29.2ab). Evening dress of silver lamé and gray tulle. French, 1938. Designed by Vionnet. Gift of Mrs. Harrison Williams, Lady Mendl, and Mrs. Ector Munn, 1946 (CI 46.4.24ab)

Inset, p. 59: Photograph by Hoyningen-Huene from *Harper's Bazaar* (September 15, 1939)

P. 59: Evening dress of ivory satin trimmed in black velvet appliqué. French, 1939. Designed by Balenciaga. Gift of Mrs. John Chambers Hughes, 1958 (CI 58.34.21ab)

P. 60, left to right: Ball gown (Venus) of gray silk tulle embroidered with feather-shaped paillettes. French, 1949. Label: Christian Dior, Paris. Gift of Mrs. Byron C. Foy, 1953 (CI 53.40.7a–e). Ball gown (Junon) of pale blue tulle embroidered with iridescent sequins. French, 1949. Label: Christian Dior, Paris. Gift of Mrs. Byron C. Foy, 1953 (CI 53.40.5a–e)

P. 61, left to right: Evening dress of plum gray and shocking-pink silk worn with yellow satin gloves. French, 1951. Label: Schiaparelli, 21 Place Vendôme, Paris. Gift of Schiaparelli, 1951 (CI 51.110.1,2ab). Evening dress of shocking-pink silk satin bodice embroidered with black beads; black silk faille skirt. French, 1953. Label: Schiaparelli. Gift of Alma De Luce, 1975 (1975.139.1ab)

P. 62, left to right: Evening dress of red wool knit. American, 1954. Designed by Traina-Norell. Gift of Mr. and Mrs. Richard V. Hare, 1976 (1976.372.3ab). Dinner dress of black crepe printed with red and white horse. American, 1945. Label: Adrian Original. Gift of Gilbert Adrian, 1945 (CI 45.94). Evening ensemble: dress of black wool jersey, belt of red leather and black wool pom-poms; coat of red and black striped velvet. American, 1937. Gift of Claire McCardell, 1949 (CI 49.37.5abc)

P. 63, left to right: Evening dress of white satin and faille trimmed with black velvet. American, 1953. Label: Charles James, 1953. Gift of Elizabeth Fairall, 1953 (CI 53.73). Evening dress of black velvet and white silk faille. American, 1953. Label: Charles James '53 Depinna. Gift of E. J. Taylor, 1975 (1975.185)

PHOTOGRAPHY

All photographs of Metropolitan Museum costumes on mannequins by Sheldan Collins. Back cover, p. 22 (right): Walter J. F. Yee, Metropolitan Museum of Art Photograph Studio. P. 13: Collections des musées d'Arles. Photography by B. Delgado. P. 16: Courtesy of the Board of Trustees of the Victoria and Albert Museum. P. 20: Metropolitan Museum of Art Photograph Studio. Pp. 25, 49, 53 (left): Gene C. Herbert, Metropolitan Museum of Art Photograph Studio. P. 49: Courtesy of Mrs. Donald M. Lovejoy (Winifred W. Lovejoy). P. 59: Copyright © 1939 by The Hearst Corporation. Courtesy of *Harper's Bazaar*. Photography by Hoyningen-Huene. Microphotography: Judith Jerde, Costume Institute, Metropolitan Museum.

Costume preparation and conservation: Judith Jerde, Associate Conservator; Costume Institute Conservation Volunteers.

Mannequin preparation and dressing: Joell Kunath.